Shielded in Dignity™

A Cyber Safety Workbook for Seasoned Citizens and Their Loved Ones

Presented By:

BLACKCREST
CYBER
RESILIENCE FORGED AT CYBER'S EDGE

Shielded in Dignity™: A Cyber Safety Workbook for Seasoned Citizens and Their Loved Ones

Published by BlackCrest Cyber, LLC An imprint of InkSpire Media. First published in the United States.

Printed in the United States of America

ISBN: (print): 979-8-9854322-1-3

Special discounts are available on bulk quantity purchases by book clubs, associations, and special interest groups. For details email: theresiliencetransformer@gmail.com or call (202) 930-3108. For information go to blackcrestcyber.com.

LEGAL NOTICE AND DISCLAIMER

This workbook is an educational resource intended solely for educational and informational purposes **only.** It is published by **BlackCrest Cyber, LLC** as part of its *Shielded in Dignity™* community awareness initiative.

The material contained herein is provided for informational purposes only and is **not** intended as a substitute for professional cybersecurity, legal, or financial advice. The exercises and strategies described are designed to raise awareness and encourage safe digital habits; they are not guaranteed to prevent cybercrime, fraud, or data loss.

Implementation of any security measures, technologies, or advice contained herein should be done with the advice of the device manufacturer. The authors and publishers are not responsible for results arising from independent implementation or interpretation of these materials.

References or links to third-party websites, products, or services (such as VirusTotal.com or AARP resources) are provided for convenience and informational purposes only. **BlackCrest Cyber, LLC** does not endorse, control, or assume responsibility for their accuracy, security, or content.

While every effort has been made to ensure accuracy and relevance at the time of publication, **BlackCrest Cyber, LLC**, **Dr. Cynthia Sutherland**, and associated partners assume no liability for any loss or damage resulting from reliance on this material or participation in related programs. The author and affiliated entities shall not be held liable for any direct, indirect, incidental, or consequential damages arising from the use of, or reliance on, this workbook or any associated materials, workshops, or online resources.

Readers are responsible for verifying that any steps or tools they implement comply with local laws and personal or organizational policies. Cybersecurity practices evolve rapidly; readers should verify all guidance and data sources for current accuracy before applying them.

WELCOME STORY

Before We Begin...

"The Moment Everything Changed"

Margaret never thought of herself as "a technology person." She used her phone to call family, her tablet to read the news, and her laptop to pay a few bills — nothing complicated. She didn't need the newest gadgets. She just wanted things to work.

One evening, her friend Mrs. Daniels called in tears. Someone had tricked her into clicking a link that looked like it came from her bank. By the time she realized something was wrong, money was missing and her email was locked.

Margaret listened quietly.
When she hung up, she whispered to herself:

"If it could happen to her... it could happen to me."

She sat at her kitchen table staring at her tablet, suddenly unsure about the digital world she thought she understood.

The next morning, she attended a community workshop — not to become a tech expert, but to feel *in control* again.

And what she found surprised her.

The instructor didn't talk down to anyone.
No one rolled their eyes at "simple" questions.
Nobody was expected to know everything.

Instead, the class began with a message that felt like a deep breath:

**"You already have the wisdom and instincts you need.
We're just adding a few modern tools."**

Margaret felt her shoulders relax.

Each lesson was short.
Each step made sense.
Each story felt familiar.

By the end of the workshop, she wasn't scared anymore.
She told her daughter later that day:

"I didn't learn everything...but I learned what matters."

This workbook is built the same way. Clear guidance you can follow at your own pace. Exercises you can complete alone or with someone you trust. Lessons that use both your life experience and your common sense.

You don't need to memorize every term.
You don't need to be a "computer person."
You don't need to feel rushed or embarrassed.

You simply need curiosity, calm, and a willingness to try one new habit at a time.

By the time you finish, you'll understand what to look for, what to avoid, and what to do — without fear or confusion. Most of all, you'll realize what Margaret eventually told her Cyber Buddy:

Let's begin this journey together —
one story,
one step,
one victory
at a time.

Welcome!

This workbook was designed with *you* in mind. My goal is to empower you with the knowledge and skills you need to safely embrace the benefits of technology and help you and a trusted loved one build safe, calm digital habits. This book includes opportunities to:

- Create strong passwords and turn on multiple locks (two locks are better than one) for your accounts.
- Spot phishing and fake links before you click.
- Protect personal information and use social media safely.
- Recognize and report cybercrime quickly (IC3.gov, IdentityTheft.gov).
- Understand today's A.I. basics and deepfakes.
- Build a Family Safe Word for emergencies.

You already have the courage, wisdom, and life experience to protect what matters most — your peace, your privacy, and your people. Together, we'll turn confusion into confidence. —

Let's embark on this journey together and unlock a world of connection, information, and new possibilities!

Dr. Cynthia Sutherland

For educational awareness only. Following the practices described in this workbook does not guarantee prevention of cybercrime, fraud, or data loss.

How to Use This Book

This workbook is your key to understanding and utilizing the power of technology, regardless of your experience level. We will focus on digital safety, making the digital world more accessible and enjoyable for you.

🧭 How This Workbook Is Organized

Each Cyber Byte is a short, focused lesson with:

- What to Know (plain-language guidance)
- What to Do (step-by-step safety actions)
- Buddy Exercise (learn together)
- Remember Anchor (a short phrase to help it stick)
- Checklist (finish and feel accomplished)

Following the strategies and checklists provided does not guarantee immunity from cybercrime, data loss, or fraud. These exercises are intended to build awareness, not serve as a substitute for comprehensive cybersecurity systems, insurance, or professional monitoring.

Reality Check

Every year, the FBI's Internet Crime Complaint Center (IC3.gov) tracks how cybercriminals target Americans. The numbers are rising — especially among adults over 60.

- **Number of complaints in 2024:** 147,127
- **Reported Losses:** $4.88B
- **Investment & crypto scams:** $1.83B lost.
- **Tech support scams:** $982M lost.
- **Romance scams:** $389M lost.
- **Average loss per senior:** $83,000.
- **Crypto-related scams doubled among those 60+.**

It's never your fault. Scammers are professionals. Understanding the risks is the first step to protecting yourself. Remember, knowledge is power!

Keep reading and arm yourself against cyber threats.

You've got this!

Meet Your Trusted Cyber Buddy

Learning is easier together. Invite a friend, family member, or caregiver to partner with you.

- Write their info: name, what they're good at, what they want to learn, their motto.
- Do Buddy Exercises together in each lesson.
- Set a Monthly Tech Check (e.g., "First Friday") to practice updates, reboots, and reviews.

Let's personalize this journey!

Fill in the blanks below to create your own Cyber Buddy profile.

My Cyber Buddy's Name: ___________________________________

One thing my Cyber Buddy is good at:

____

One thing my Cyber Buddy wants to learn:

____

Tip: Treat your Cyber Buddy as a reminder to stay vigilant and practice safe online habits!

🔐CYBER BYTE 1: Don't Go Crazy. Get Creative.

The Password That Became the Key to Everything

Uncle Terry liked to keep things simple.
He used the same password for almost everything — his email, his pharmacy account, even his favorite game app.
It was the name of his childhood street: "WestEnd55."
Easy to remember.
Never failed him.

One morning, Uncle Terry logged into his email and saw something unusual.
A message he didn't recognize.
Then another.
Then a notification saying his password had been changed.

His stomach dropped.

He called his niece, Cynthia, the unofficial "tech helper" of the family. She asked him gently:

"Uncle Terry... have you used that same password anywhere else?"

He paused, then nodded slowly.

Cynthia smiled — a kind smile, not a judgmental one.

“Then someone probably guessed it.
But don’t worry. We can fix this.”

Together, they created a new password using a simple memory trick.
Not a random jumble of symbols — a phrase tied to something Terry loved: fishing at Blue Ridge Lake.

They turned that memory into a strong password:
Bluer!dg3F!sh!ng2025

“That’s a long one,” he laughed.
Cynthia said, “That’s the point. Longer is stronger.”

Then she helped him turn on MFA — Multi-Factor Authentication — the second lock on for the account.

Now, even if someone tried to guess his new password, they’d also need the code sent to his phone.

A week later, Uncle Terry told his neighbor:

“I didn’t become a computer expert.
I just added a deadbolt.”

And just like that, he wasn’t scared of passwords anymore.
He understood them.
And more importantly — he felt protected.

Password Protection

Think of passwords as the key to your digital castle. Stolen or weak passwords remain a leading cause of account compromise. But a strong password is only your first lock — the second lock is Multi-Factor Authentication (MFA).

Together, they make your digital doors twice as hard to break.

Passwords: What makes a strong password?

- At least 12 characters long
- A mix of uppercase and lowercase letters
- Includes numbers and symbols
- Is not easily guessable (avoid names, birthdays, etc.)
- Avoid using public information as your password. For example, do not use any part of your name, your address, your kids names, your pets names, or your close friends names.

Examples:

- Weak: password123 vs Better: P@sswOrd123
- Stronger:
  - *White House* → Wh!+3H0u$e!!
  - I love to walk my dog in the park → Il0vet0w@lkMyd0g!nTh3P@rk

MFA (Multi-Factor Authentication):

Think of MFA as adding an extra lock to your door. Even if someone guesses your password, they still need a second code from your phone or email to get in.

How MFA Works:

1. First, you enter your password (Lock 1).
2. Second, the company will send you a text message, email link, or fingerprint.
3. Third, confirm your identity with the **text code, email link, or fingerprint** (Lock 2).

WARNING!!! If you receive a text message or email link that you did not initiate. DO NOT CLICK ON THE LINK. Change your password and call the Company you have the account with using their official number.

Cyber Buddy Exercise

Your Favorite Place /Song /Memory/ Quote:

____

Special Characters You'll Use:

____

Your New Password Formula:

____

Create 3 12-character passwords using memory cues: favorite places, songs, or memories

1. __________________________________
2. __________________________________
3. __________________________________

Test password strength and note preferably in Your Cyber Logbook.

Checklist: Password Security

- Change Default passwords on all devices and accounts at least every 6 months.
- Enable Multi-Factor Authentication on all accounts
  - Email
  - Online Banking
  - Social Media Accounts

- Healthcare Portal

Ask your trusted Cyber Buddy to help set it up on your devices, if needed.

Have your partner read your new password formula back to you and confirm MFA is turned on together — teamwork builds memory *and* safety.

REMEMBER *Two locks are better than one.*

Next Steps:

Great job completing Cyber Byte #1! You've taken the first step toward building a safer digital home. Next, we'll explore how to keep your **devices** updated, healthy, and protected.

🔐CYBER BYTE 2:
Don't Ignore. Install.

The Update She Didn't Think She Needed

Pastor Theresa loved starting her mornings with a warm cup of tea and a quick scroll through her tablet. Recipes, church announcements, and photos from her grandkids filled her screen like sunshine.

But one thing she *always* avoided?

A little box that kept appearing:

"Software Update Available. Install Now?"

Each time, she tapped **"Not Now."**
Not because she didn't care—but because she was afraid an update might change something she couldn't fix.

Then one afternoon, her favorite puzzle app froze.
Her music wouldn't open.
And her tablet slowed to a crawl.

Frustrated, she called her friend Miss Shirley—the neighborhood's unofficial "tech whisperer."

Miss Shirley arrived with her usual smile and said, "Theresa, your tablet isn't broken... it's just waiting for the updates you've been skipping."

Theresa blinked.
"Updates?"

"Yep," Miss Shirley said, tapping the update button. "These updates fix problems, close security holes, and keep everything running smoothly. Have you been clicking 'later' for months."

Pastor Theresa embarrassingly responded with a small smirk, "Yessss".

Shirley clicked **Update Now**. In minutes, the tablet perked up as if someone had flipped a switch.

Then she turned on **Automatic Updates**, rebooted the Wi-Fi router, and showed Theresa how to keep her devices healthy with simple monthly habits.

By the time she left, Theresa wasn't confused—she was confident.

A big improvement.
A calmer, safer digital life.

5-Step Checklist to Secure Your Devices

Just like your home, your devices need regular maintenance to stay secure and running smoothly. Ignoring updates and basic upkeep can leave you vulnerable to cyber threats. Don't let this happen to you!

1. **Back Up Photos:** Save important photos and documents to the cloud or a USB drive.
2. **Update Your Phone, Tablet, and Computer:** Install the latest software updates.
3. **Reboot Your Wi-Fi Router Monthly:** Think of it as a fresh start for your internet.
4. **Use Automatic Updates:** Let your devices update themselves automatically (if possible).
5. **Delete Old Apps:** Remove apps you no longer use.

Let's do these actions at least 1 time per month as a regular habit!

Cyber Buddy Exercise

Talk with your Cyber Buddy (a friend, family member, or fellow workshop participant) about the following:

1. Turn On Auto-Update

Check your phone, tablet, and computer to ensure automatic updates are enabled.

---

2. Choose Your Monthly Reboot Day

Pick a day you'll remember. Examples:

- First Sunday

- Payday Friday
- The 1st of every month

Our Reboot Day:

---

3. Delete Three Apps You Don't Use

Cleaner device = safer device.

Apps I deleted:

1. ______
2. ______
3. ______

4. Update Check

With your Cyber Buddy, confirm together:

- ☐ Updates installed?
- ☐ Router rebooted recently?
- ☐ Apps cleaned up?
- ☐ Photos backed up?

Keeping your devices updated and maintained is crucial for protecting yourself from cyber threats.

REMEMBER Restart to stay smart!

Next Steps:

Congratulations! Keep practicing these skills and remember to stay vigilant online. The next lesson will cover phishing scams and how to spot them. Stay tuned.

CYBER BYTE 3:
Watch Out for Sneaky LINKS.

The Text That Looked Real Enough to Believe

Ms. Doris was expecting a package — a small birthday gift she ordered for her grandson. She checked the tracking earlier in the week, so when a text message buzzed on her phone saying:

"Your package is delayed. Click here to update delivery info."

...it didn't seem strange at all.

She opened the message and almost tapped the link, but something tugged at her attention.

The number wasn't a real phone number — just a strange string of digits.
The message didn't mention any company name.
Not UPS.
Not USPS.
Not Amazon.

Still, she didn't want her grandson's gift to go missing.
Her finger hovered above the blue link.

Just then, her friend Mr. Lee walked into the community room and noticed her hesitant expression.

"What's that?" he asked.

"A delivery delay notice," she replied. "I just need to update my address."

Mr. Lee took the phone gently and zoomed in on the message.

The word *delivery* was misspelled.
The link ended in **".co.ru"** — not **".com."**
The number didn't match any delivery company.

"That's a sneaky one," he said. "They want you to click fast so you don't think."

Ms. Doris set the phone down slowly and opened her real Amazon app — her package was perfectly on schedule.
No delays.
No problems.
No missing gift.

She sighed in relief.
"That almost got me."

Mr. Lee smiled.
"It almost gets all of us. The trick is not rushing."

That afternoon, Doris made herself a promise:

If a message surprises me, I pause.
If a link looks odd, I check.
If something feels off, I won't click — I'll verify instead.

From that day on, she never tapped a suspicious link again.

Phishing scams were the **1 reported crime type** in 2024 — over **193,000 complaints** ($70M losses). Scammers want you to click fast and think slow.

Scammers try to rush you so you don't think clearly. 🙅 Don't let them!

Common Red Flags:

🚫 Urgent or threatening language (Act now! Your account will be closed!)
🧾 Misspelled company names or email addresses
🔗 Suspicious links or attachments
💰 Requests for money, gift cards, or personal info
⏱️ Unusual timing (middle of the night messages)

Cyber Buddy Exercise

Here's how to protect yourself from phishing scams:

1. **Don't panic!** 🚨 Scammers use alarming messages to scare you into clicking. If a message creates a sense of urgency, be cautious.
2. **Check the sender's address.** 👀 Don't just look at the name. Verify the full email address or phone number.
3. **Hover before you click.** 🖱 On your computer, hover your mouse over the link to see the actual URL. Does it look suspicious?
4. **Call to verify.** 📞 If something feels off, call the person or company directly to confirm.
5. **Use VirusTotal.** Use a tool like VirusTotal.com to test suspicious links.

Explain *why* a message is fake in their own words. Teaching it back reinforces recognition and long-term memory.

REMEMBER	✋ Pause before you click — that's the CyberSmart trick. *Pause. Verify. Delete.*

Next Steps:

Congratulations on completing the third Cyber Byte! Keep practicing these skills and remember to stay vigilant online. The next lesson will cover Artificial Intelligence. Stay tuned.

CYBER BYTE 4:
Seeing Isn't Always Believing

The Voice That Was Almost Too Real

Mr. Caroline was chopping vegetables for dinner when her phone rang.
The caller ID said **Private Number**, but the voice on the line made her heart stop.

"Grandma... it's me. I'm in trouble. Please don't tell Mom."

It sounded exactly like her grandson Jordan.
Same tone. Same rhythm. Same little breathy pause between sentences.
It was so perfect that for a moment, she didn't even question it.

"What's wrong, sweetheart?" she asked, gripping the counter.

The voice came back shaky and urgent.
"I need help. Please send money right away. I can't explain everything now—"

Helen felt panic rising, but something didn't fit.

Jordan always called her **Gram**, not Grandma.
He never said "please don't tell Mom."
And he certainly didn't rush her like this.

Her instincts whispered:
Slow down. Something isn't right.

She took a deep breath and said calmly,
"Jordan, tell me our family phrase."

There was silence.
A long, uncomfortable silence.

Then the voice hung up.

Her hands trembled as she called Jordan's real number — the one saved in her contacts.
He answered immediately, laughing with friends in the background.

"Gram! What's up?"

Helen sank into a chair, relieved and angry all at once.

"Someone copied your voice," she said. "Perfectly."

Jordan went quiet.
"A.I. can do that now," he said. "But they can't copy our memories."

Together they chose a **family safe word**, something only the two of them would ever know.
They practiced it twice, then promised to check in more often.

Helen hung up feeling something she didn't expect —
not fear... but confidence.

Artificial Intelligence (A.I.) — In Plain Language

What Is A.I.?

Artificial Intelligence (A.I.) just means computers using data and math to make smart guesses.

You already use A.I. when you:

- Ask Alexa or Siri a question
- Get movie or music suggestions from Google Chrome using Gemini
- Use chatbots to get help online

Most AI is helpful and safe.

What Is Generative A.I.?

Generative A.I. is A.I. that can *create* new things — like words, pictures, or music.

Examples:

- Writing letters or recipes
- Making images or graphics
- Composing simple music

Think of it as a digital artist or writer that learned from many examples.

Wise Tip:
Generative A.I. can sound very confident, even when it's wrong — always double-check important information.

What Are Deepfakes?

Most people use AI for good things. But some use it to create fake videos, photos, or voices that look and sound real.

These are called deepfakes.

A deepfake is:

- A video, picture, or voice recording
- Changed or created by A.I.
- Designed to trick you

5 Quick Ways to Check a Deepfake

1. 👀 **Look closely.** Does the face move strangely? Do lips match the words?
2. 🔊 **Listen.** Does the voice sound flat, robotic, or slightly “off”?
3. 🌫 **Check the picture.** Do shadows, lighting, or background look wrong?
4. 🕵 **Check the source.** Who posted it? Is it a trusted account?
5. 🔗 **Verify before sharing.** Search the story on real news sites.

Common Examples

Type	Description	What You Can Do
1. Voice Cloning Scam	A scammer uses AI to copy your loved one's voice and call asking for money.	Hang up and call your loved one back directly on the number you have for them or another loved one.
2. Celebrity Investment Ad	A deepfake of a famous person promoting crypto or miracle products.	No celebrity will ever ask you for money online. Even so, check their official celebrity channels for confirmation OR verify through official channels; do not send money or meet strangers.
3. Fake News Videos	Altered clips of public figures designed to cause fear or	Verify the story using at least 2 reputable news outlets before sharing.

	anger.	
4. Romance Deepfakes	Scammers use fake images or videos to build false emotional connections.	Be cautious of people who are "too perfect" too fast. Don't download images from sources you have never met.

🧰 Safety Checklist

Technology may copy your **voice**, but not your **wisdom**. Use your instincts first.

✓ Verify unknown calls before sending money or information.

✓ Create and use a **family safe word** for emergencies.

✓ Avoid clicking unfamiliar links or downloading new apps from untrusted sources or strangers.

✓ Get news from trusted sources (BBC, Reuters, PBS, AP).

✓ Talk about suspicious messages or videos with your **Cyber Buddy** before reacting.

Cyber Buddy Exercise

Family Safe Word Exercise

Work with your Cyber Buddy or family to create a private, easy-to-remember word or phrase that only your family knows.

How It Works:

If someone calls, texts, or emails claiming to be a loved one in trouble — ask for the **safe word** before taking any action.

Step	Task	Notes
1	Choose your word or phrase (something not obvious, like a favorite memory or nickname).	Example: *Sunflower 42*
2	Write it down and share it only with trusted family.	Never text or email it. Say it in person.
3	Practice using it in your monthly Tech Check with your Cyber Buddy.	Review together and confirm everyone remembers.

Write Below:

Our Family Safe Word:

____

Who Knows It:

____

Protect Yourself with Technology

- Use Caller ID and call-blocking apps (Hiya, Nomorobo, or your phone's built-in spam filter).
- Enable multifactor authentication on all major accounts.
- Adjust privacy settings on Facebook, YouTube, and social media to control who can tag or message you.
- Keep your software and devices updated — AI-powered scams often exploit outdated systems.

Write Below:

One thing I'll do differently when I see shocking news or videos online:

____

One person I'll share this lesson with:

____

REMEMBER	*If your gut says something's off — pause before you post.*

Next Steps: Congratulations on completing the fourth Cyber Byte! Keep practicing these skills and remember to stay vigilant online. The next lesson will focus on Reporting and Recovery. Stay tuned.

🔐CYBER BYTE 5:
When in Doubt, Report Out.

What This Lesson Is Really About

If something feels wrong — a strange phone call, a pop-up, a weird message, a charge you don't recognize — the **fastest and safest** thing you can do is **tell someone right away**.

Reporting early can:

- stop scammers
- freeze stolen money
- help recover funds
- protect your account
- prevent others from being harmed

You are not "bothering" anyone.
You are doing exactly what banks and agencies want you to do.

Simple Steps to Take If You Think You've Been Scammed

1. Call Your Bank First

Use the number on the *back of your card* or your last statement. Not a number sent in a text or popup.

Tell them: "I think I may be dealing with a scam."

Your bank can:

- freeze your card
- block a payment
- start a recovery process
- walk you through next steps

---

2. Report Online Scams to IC3.gov

This is the FBI's Internet Crime Complaint Center.

They will ask for:

- what happened
- dates
- amounts
- any screenshots or details

You will get a **case number**. Keep it in a safe place.

---

3. Let One Trusted Person Know

This step is about support, memory, and clarity.

Tell your:

- Cyber Buddy

For educational awareness only. Following the practices described in this workbook does not guarantee prevention of cybercrime, fraud, or data loss.

- family member
- neighbor
- trusted friend

Talking about what happened helps you stay calm and remember what steps you've already taken.

A Few Helpful Notes

- Scammers often try to create panic. Slow down.
- You don't need proof — just suspicion.
- Early reporting leads to the best chance of fund recovery.
- Even if it's too late to get all the money back, reporting helps stop the scammer from hurting someone else.

Cyber Buddy Exercise

With your Cyber Buddy:

1. Fill Out These Contacts in Large Print

My Bank:

Fraud Department:

IC3.gov Case Number (if any):

My Trusted Person:

---

2. Practice a Mock Report

Walk through what you *would* say if you needed to report a scam.
This builds confidence and reduces panic during a real situation.

REMEMBER	✋ *When in doubt, report out.*

Next Steps:

Congratulations on completing the fifth Cyber Byte! Keep practicing these skills and remember to stay vigilant online. The next lesson will focus on staying safe when you do not have Internet. Stay tuned

🔐 CYBER BYTE 6: Staying Safe Without the Internet

You Don't Need Wi-Fi to Be Cyber Smart

You may not use a smartphone, apps, or the internet — and that's okay.
Scammers still try phone calls, letters, and door-to-door tricks.
But you already have the strongest tools you need:

Your instincts.
Your patience.
Your community.

Let's keep things simple.

---

1. The Knock at the Door

A stranger shows up claiming to be from:

- a utility company
- a charity
- a repair service

...and wants money or access right away.

Your rule:
No decisions at the door.

Say:
"Please leave your information. I will call the office myself."

This one sentence keeps both you and your money safe.

---

2. The Scary Phone Call

Someone calls saying:

- your Social Security number is in danger
- your bank account is locked
- your grandchild is in trouble

These calls are designed to **panic you**.

Hang up.
Call the real number on your **bank card**, **Social Security letter**, or **trusted contact list**.

If the real office says everything is fine, you can breathe again.

---

3. The "Official" Letter

A letter arrives with:

- a government logo
- a demand for payment
- or a threat of fines

Check for:

- misspelled words
- no return address
- pressure to act quickly

Take the letter to your post office or county office. They'll tell you if it's real.

---

4. Protecting Your Money (Without Technology)

A few simple habits keep your money safe:

Paying bills:
Use the address printed on the official bill.

Storing checks:
Keep them in a locked drawer or ask for direct deposit.

Tracking accounts:
Ask your bank to call you if they see something unusual.

Lost card:
Always call the number on the **back of your card**, never a number from a caller.

Cyber Buddy Exercise

With your Cyber Buddy:

Build Your Safety Circle

Choose 2–3 people you trust.
These are the people you call **before** you make a financial decision.

My Safety Circle:

1. ____________________
2. ____________________
3. ____________________

Create a simple **safe word** for emergencies — something only you know.

Your promise to each other:
"No one makes a quick decision alone."

Post Your Emergency Numbers

Write these in large print and place near your phone:

Local Sheriff: ______________________
Bank Fraud Line: ____________________
AARP Fraud Watch: 1-877-908-3360
FTC Scam Reporting: 1-877-382-4357
County Aging Office: _________________

Seeing this list every day gives peace of mind.

Share What You've Learned

At church, the market, or the senior center, people often talk about strange calls or letters.

Share your new rule:

"Pause before you pay. Verify before you trust."

You become a protector — not a target.

🧰 Shielded in Dignity™ Checklist

✓ I verified before giving money or information.

✓ I hung up on a suspicious caller.

✓ I talked with someone in my Safety Circle.

✓ I shredded old mail or added a mailbox lock.

✓ I shared a safety tip with a friend.

Each check is a victory — proof that wisdom, not Wi-Fi, is your strongest defense.

REMEMBER	✋ Trust your instincts, not their urgency.

Next Steps:

Congratulations! Keep practicing these skills and remember to stay vigilant online. The next lesson will focus on Bitcoin and Scams. Stay tuned

CYBER BYTE 7: Safety with Digital Money

The Bitcoin Trick That Almost Worked

Mr. Marvin, an 83-year-old husband in Colorado, was reading a normal news article when a big red pop-up suddenly took over his screen.

"Your computer has a virus. Call Microsoft Support now."

It looked official. It sounded urgent.
The popup told him to fix the problem **immediately**.

Wanting to protect his computer, Marvin called the number.

On the phone, the person acted polite and professional. He asked Marvin to go to a website and click on a link to install the latest updates. Things quickly escalated. Marvin watched as the person took control of his computer. Then, the person informed Marvin of an error with his bank account. So, he told Marvin to log into his bank account to check. As Marvin was checking his bank account, the person on the computer quietly moved money from savings to checking.

The person pressured Marvin to withdraw cash and instructed Marvin to deposit the cash into a Bitcoin ATM at 7-Eleven

Marvin had never even heard of "Bitcoin ATMs."
But the scammer used urgency, fear, and fast instructions to keep him confused.

Fortunately, his wife asked, "hey honey, what's wrong". He explained "That she wouldn't understand. He was doing some James Bond stuff with Microsoft and the Bank."

She stepped in and called the number on the back of their real bank card, not the number on the pop-up.

The bank employee said immediately:

"Hang up. This is a scam."

Her quick thinking saved them $6,000.

This wasn't a story about "falling for something."
It was a reminder of how convincing these scams have become — and how much scammers rely on Bitcoin to steal money fast.

What Is Bitcoin (Plain & Simple)?

Bitcoin is digital money.
There are:

- no bills
- no coins
- no banks

You buy Bitcoin through:

- apps (like CashApp, Coinbase)
- websites
- Bitcoin ATMs in gas stations & convenience stores

Once you send Bitcoin, you cannot get it back.
There is no customer service and no refunds — ever.

That is why scammers love it.

Why Scammers Push Bitcoin

Scammers use Bitcoin because:

1. It's instant.

Money moves in seconds — before you even realize what happened.

2. It can't be reversed.

Unlike bank transactions, you cannot cancel a Bitcoin payment.

3. It confuses people.

Most people don't fully understand it, and scammers take advantage of that confusion.

4. It looks "techy."

Seniors often think Bitcoin is something only banks or tech companies understand — scammers use that to sound convincing.

Clear Rule:

If anyone tells you to use Bitcoin, it's a scam.
No exceptions.
No "special cases."
No emergencies.

If you hear any of these phrases:

✓ "Buy Bitcoin to fix the issue."

✓ "We need you to use a Bitcoin ATM."

✓ "Convert your money to crypto to protect it."

✓ "This is the fastest way to stop the fraud."

It is 100% a scam.

Real banks, real companies, and real government agencies will never ask you to pay in Bitcoin.

The 10-Second Rescue Plan

If a pop-up or caller ever directs you toward cryptocurrency:

✓ 1. Close the pop-up.

This is not a real alert.
Your computer is *not* infected.
The message itself *is* the scam.

✓ 2. Do NOT call any number you see on your screen.

Scammers place their own numbers in pop-ups.

✓ 3. Call your bank using the number on your debit/credit card.

Only use numbers you trust.

✓ 4. Get a second pair of eyes.

Ask your Cyber Buddy, spouse, or a family member.

A calm person looking over your shoulder can save thousands.

Quick Safety Checklist

✓ I will never send money using Bitcoin.
✓ I will never use a Bitcoin ATM under pressure.
✓ I will close pop-ups telling me to call support.
✓ I will use the number on my bank card — not a screen or text.

✓ I will tell a trusted person before sending any money.

✓ I know Bitcoin transactions cannot be reversed.

Cyber Buddy Exercise

Reflection Activity:

1. What would I do if a pop-up warned me my computer was infected?

   ____

2. Who is the first person I would call to double-check?

   ____

3. If a stranger pressured me to "act now," what would I do?

   ____

REMEMBER	Stay alert. Stay calm. When in doubt—hang up and verify.

Next Steps:

Congratulations! Keep practicing these skills and remember to stay vigilant online. The next lesson will address the shame and embarrassment of being a victim.

Fraud & Feelings

Why Scams Affect More Than Just Our Money

Fraud isn't only about stolen dollars or tricky technology. It touches something much deeper — our confidence, our routines, and how safe we feel in our own lives.

And almost every scam begins the same way:
with pressure, fear, confusion, or a sudden sense of urgency.

These emotional "hooks" are designed to catch anyone:

💕 "I love you."
Used in romance scams to build false trust.

😨 "Your family member is in trouble."
Used in imposter or fake police calls.

💸 "Act fast or you'll lose money!"
Used in investment or bank scams.

💻 "Your computer is infected!"
Used in tech-support pop-ups and calls.

Here's the truth:

None of the people in these stories were foolish.
None made a silly mistake.
None lacked intelligence.

They were simply human — caring, trusting, and caught off guard for a moment.

That's what scammers rely on.

But every story in this workbook also shows something powerful:

✨ Calm is stronger than fear.

✨ Stopping to verify beats pressure.

✨ Your instincts beat intimidation.

✨ And connection — asking someone you trust — beats isolation every time.

Fraud isn't a sign of weakness.
It's a sign that you were targeted by someone skilled at emotional manipulation.

What matters most is what you do next.

🤝 Cyber Buddy Exercise

Take a moment with your Cyber Buddy to answer:

1. **How did you feel the last time you received a suspicious message?**

---

2. **What could help you stay calm next time?**

Talking about it helps your brain store the information — and helps you respond with confidence in the future.

You're not weaker for trusting.
You're wiser now for learning.

REMEMBER	✋ *If it's urgent and emotional — pause and ask for the safe word.*

Closing Section: Your Journey, Your Power

You've reached the end of *Shielded in Dignity™*, and something important has happened along the way.

You discovered that:

- You're not "bad with technology."
- The world simply changed fast — and no one slowed down to explain it clearly.
- Scammers are trained professionals, not harmless tricksters.
- You are not the problem.

With every pause, every second look, every "Let me call my bank first," you took back control.
You proved that caution, experience, and steady thinking are real strengths.

You are not an easy target.
You are a protector — and now a prepared one.

As you move forward, remember:

- You can slow things down.
- You can say "no" or hang up.
- You can verify, double-check, and take your time.

- You can protect your heart and your money with confidence.

And when you share what you've learned — at church, at the senior center, or with a friend who says, "Something strange happened yesterday" — you become a shield for someone else too.

That's what being a Cyber Guardian really means.

You are not behind.
You are not a burden.
You are wise, steady, and capable.

Stay connected.
Stay confident.
Stay shielded in dignity.

CYBER GUARDIAN PLEDGE

Your Commitment to Safe, Confident Digital Living

I pledge to protect myself online with calm, care, and confidence.
I will pause before I click, verify before I trust, and reach out when something feels wrong.

I will use the tools I've learned:

- strong passwords,
- safe browsing,
- careful clicking,
- and trusted conversations.

I will listen to my instincts and slow things down.
I will ask questions, double-check information, and take my time.

By signing below, I acknowledge my strength, my growth, and my role as a Cyber Guardian.

Signature: ______________________
Date: __________________________

💕 A Closing Message from Dr. Cynthia Sutherland

When I began creating this workbook, I had one goal: to make sure that no one, especially our seasoned citizens, would ever feel powerless in a world that's always online.

You've spent your life building wisdom — and now, that wisdom becomes your greatest security system. When you:

- *Pause before you click,*
- *Verify before you trust, and*
- *Stay connected to your* ***Cyber Buddy*** *and community — you turn fear into confidence, and vulnerability into strength.*

💡 *The Takeaway*

Older adults may be the 1 target group for online fraud — but with awareness, compassion, and the right tools, you can become the ***1 protected group*** *in the digital world.*

🦋 *My Wish for You*

May you never underestimate your power to protect what matters most — your peace, your privacy, and your people. You are not just surviving this digital age — you are mastering it.

With love and cyber confidence,
Dr. Cynthia Sutherland
Global Cybersecurity Leader

Glossary (Plain-Language)

Short, clear definitions you can trust. Terms are alphabetized. Where helpful, an example is included in parentheses.

Account Compromise – When someone breaks into your online account and uses it without permission.

Adware – Unwanted software that shows ads or redirects you to websites.

Agentic AI – AI systems that can take actions to complete tasks (e.g., schedule, send emails). They still need human oversight.

AI (Artificial Intelligence) – Computer programs that learn patterns to answer questions or create things.

AGI (Artificial General Intelligence) – A theoretical future AI that could reason broadly like a person. It does not exist today.

Anti-virus / Anti-malware – Security software that finds and blocks malicious programs.

App (Application) – A program on your phone, tablet, or computer.

App Permissions – What an app is allowed to access (camera, contacts, location). Only allow what is needed.

Attachment – A file sent with an email or text. If unexpected, don't open it.

Authentication – Proving you are you (password, code, fingerprint).

Backup – A copy of your files stored elsewhere (cloud or USB drive) in case something goes wrong.

Biometrics – Your fingerprint or face used to unlock a device.

Bluetooth – Short-range wireless connection between devices (turn off when not in use).

Bot – Automated program that can perform tasks; criminals use bots to attack accounts.

Breach (Data Breach) – When a company's data is exposed or stolen.

Browser – The program you use to access the web (Chrome, Safari, Edge, Firefox).

Browser Cache / Cookies – Small files your browser saves. Clearing them can fix sign-in or page problems.

CAPTCHA – A quick test ("I'm not a robot") to stop automated attacks.

Cloud / Cloud Storage – Files saved on the internet (Google Drive, iCloud, OneDrive) so you can access them from any device.

Credential Stuffing – Criminals try stolen passwords from one site on your other accounts.

Credit Freeze – A free tool that stops new credit from being opened in your name. Unfreeze when you need to apply.

Cyber Buddy – Your trusted partner who practices safety steps with you.

Cyber Guardian – A person who protects themselves and helps others stay safe.

Cybercrime – Any crime that uses computers, phones, or the internet.

Deepfake – AI-made or altered video, audio, or image that looks real but isn't (e.g., fake voice of a loved one).

Device – Your phone, tablet, computer, or smart gadget.

Encryption – Scrambling data so only the right person can read it.

Firewall – A security barrier that blocks suspicious network traffic.

Financial Fraud Kill Chain – A bank-to-bank process used to try to quickly recall fraudulent wire transfers (timing matters).

FTC (Federal Trade Commission) – U.S. agency that helps consumers. Their site IdentityTheft.gov guides recovery steps.

Generative AI – AI that creates text, images, audio, or video (e.g., ChatGPT, image creators).

Hotspot – A phone or device that shares its internet connection with others. Secure with a strong password.

Hover (Over a Link) – Move your mouse over a link (without clicking) to see the real website address.

IC3 (Internet Crime Complaint Center) – FBI site to report online fraud: IC3.gov.

Identity Theft – Someone uses your personal information to open accounts or steal money.

Incognito / Private Browsing – A browser mode that doesn't save history on your device (websites can still see activity).

Keylogger – Malware that records what you type.

Malware – Harmful software; includes viruses, ransomware, spyware, and more.

Ransomware: locks your files and demands payment.

- Spyware: secretly watches what you do.
- Trojan: looks harmless but contains malware.
- Worm/Virus: spreads from device to device.

MFA / 2FA (Multi-Factor Authentication) – A second step to log in (code, app, or fingerprint). Strongly recommended.

Network – How your devices connect (home Wi-Fi, office network, cellular).

Operating System (OS) – The main software on your device (Windows, macOS, iOS, Android). Keep it updated.

Passphrase – A long, easy-to-remember password made of several words plus symbols (e.g., Blue!River!Sunset!27).

Password Manager – A secure "vault" that creates and remembers strong passwords for you.

Patch / Update – A fix that closes security holes. Turn on automatic updates.

Phishing – Fake messages that try to trick you into clicking or giving information (email).

- Smishing: phishing by text message.
- Vishing: phishing by voice/call.

Pop-up – A window that appears suddenly in your browser. Don't click "fix your computer" pop-ups.

Private Information (PII) – Personal details like SSN, birthdate, address, bank numbers. Guard closely.

QR Code – A square barcode you scan with a camera to open a link. Verify the source; don't scan random codes.

Reboot / Restart – Turn a device off and on to refresh and install updates (do this for routers monthly).

Recovery Codes – Backup login codes you save when enabling MFA; store in a safe place.

Router – The box that brings internet to your home and creates Wi-Fi. Reboot monthly; change default password.

Safe Word (Family) – A private word your family uses to confirm identity in emergencies.

Scam – A trick to steal money or information. Common forms: fake tech support, romance, investment, government imposters.

Screenshot – A picture of what's on your screen; helpful for reporting fraud.

SIM Swap – Criminal moves your phone number to their SIM card to intercept codes. Ask your carrier for a port-out PIN.

Social Engineering – Tricking people using emotion (fear, love, urgency) instead of hacking computers.

Spam – Unwanted messages or ads.

Spoofing – Faking caller ID, email address, or website to look legitimate.

SSID – Your Wi-Fi network name (e.g., "SmithHome-5G").

Strong Password – 12+ characters, mixed letters/numbers/symbols, unique for each account.

URL (Web Address) – The line at the top of the browser (e.g., https://example.com). Check for spelling and padlock.

VPN (Virtual Private Network) – An app that encrypts your internet connection, especially useful on public Wi-Fi.

VirusTotal – Free website to check if a link or file is risky: virustotal.com.

Wi-Fi – Your wireless internet connection at home or in public.

Zelle / P2P Payments – Instant money transfer services. Treat like cash—only send to people you know.

www.ingramcontent.com/pod-product-compliance
Lightning Source LLC
LaVergne TN
LVHW060044210926
848481LV00013B/3951